To Micha

Fish say
That's only most of the iceberg

Enjoy!

Alan Wolfson

Contents

Just A Pedestrian Wearing A Car

Do not go mental into that green light.
Upon sight of the walking figure,
walk at a walking pace.
It is not a signal to trigger the start of a race.

Nor an order for subordinates to scurry.
Some commander demands ya hurry up -
Sitting there, hand-brake primed behind their wheel.

Take your time.

Notice the motorist is just a pedestrian
lording it up on their throne like they own the tar.

Just a pedestrian dressed in pressed steel.

Just a pedestrian wearing a car.

The Softest Working Man In Show Business

It's odd that you shove and you prod with impunity
A well respected pillow of the community.
You're pushing the cushion and poking the pack
And burying your fingers, but he springs right back.

Try more 'fluffy slipper', less 'give it some welly'
When indulging the bulging of buttock and belly.
There's plenty of give in, it doesn't take much.
He's so easy squeezy, he's such a soft touch.

He's a puff of air off a whirling fan.
Like a tuft of hair -
The softest working man in show business.

The velvet curtain goes up to reveal
A pneumatic asthmatic as round as a wheel,
As he takes to the stage in a blaze of blancmange,
All rubbery putty and marshmallow sponge.

His headdress is more a chinchilla fedora,
With poncho and panties in matching angora.
The spotlight is mango, the footlights are peach.
He soft-shoe-shuffles like the sand on a beach,
Increasingly creasing up in creases after
folding over in folds of laughter.

Dilating the breath of inflatable doll, it
emerges a plethora of vapour and jollity.

A puff of air off a whirling fan,
Like a tuft of hair -
He's the softest working man in show business.

The n at the end of autumn

Autumn. Autumnal.
Autumn nil, Winter won.
Leaves lost to the wind and the dwindling sun.

The gravid wood is well hung.
Foliage falls forfeit to great holes of sky and perforations amalgamate.
Chinks of light coalesce and settle around thinning arms.
Cover is blown, exposing silhouettes of nests sketched
like shadows on a scanned lung.

A fresh breath of air chases and fluctuates.
Branches articulate, gesticulate.
Squalls and gusty blows burst erratic bouquets of flakes,
all bluster and histrionics.
Chaotic flocks fall filigree, acrobatic, and theatrical.
A spectacle of balletic freckles filling the sky
like persistent mischief menacing a snow globe.

Shed loads of shedding leaves leave in vain swagger
as the umber cloak disrobes, deciduous and run ragged.
Trunk and branch and twig remain
anatomies that are trees arteries and veins.

The reluctant last cling and rust autumnal, or tumble to earth,
to enlist with their crisp ephemeral
red and yellow fellows unsettled on the floor.
Suddenly they scurry, spooked. Then still once more,
fugitive between vortex wheels, and turbulent scatterings-about.

Once rain cramps the devil, the damp can't dance.
Soggy pavements and soused paths
press the little ginger buggers into découpage.
The sun swings low with fallen crest. Shadows lengthen and days shorten.
Unruffled carpets are laid to rest,
Dormant as the n at the end of Autumn.

My Convex Is Your Concave

The way a serrated edge
fits the bits that are missing.
The way tyre treads match every track they engrave,
We keep fitting together like tongue and groove. Listen,
My convex is your concave.

Hey misbehave - meet misdemeanour,
Never seen a keener couple since Tex met Mex.
We got the bottle to topple a window cleaner
Catching me concave and you convex.

We keep fitting together like tongue and groove.
Like skin in tight leather with no room to move.
Lucky seven and snake eyes the rough with the smooth.
You've got nothing to fake, I've got nothing to prove.

We band like a spoon in a spoon in a spoon.
Like the hands on a clock face at midnight and noon.
When serendipity flips opportune
Then the whole of the Sun is eclipsed by the Moon.

We keep fitting together like Roger and Wilco,
Like Top Cat and Bilko, like peaches and cream
We seem to be seamless, like Velcro and Velcro.
I go to a go-go, you shake a tambourine.

No lover of green

What does an orange do?
The citrus orb sits there absorbing blue.
Likewise a lime takes time to relax
while it
extracts violet.
(That purple people-eater fellow
is not so much depleting people as eating yellow)

Colours detected are what's left behind, reflected,
less the rest of the spectrum that's been removed.
And a reflective mood is easier
with synaesthesia.

Take blue.
Miserable.
Is there a bul-ue
that's not been bruised by the brickbats?
While the bouquets have all been
mounting up on the green.
Because green is blessed.
And the thing is, I guess, blue's had a bad press.

So lose the blues, let's go with chartreuse.
It's good, it's clean, it's racing green.
It's Lincoln, it's olive, it's lime, it's marine.
It's pine, it's jade, it's a gorgeous emerald shade.
Stick with us. Ubiquitous GREEN.

How green was my valley? How green are my sleeves?
And how green grow the rushes, or so everyone believes . . . .
But green deceives your eyes.
So when surmising the vegetation,
It's surprising to discover the scenery is no lover of green.
The pigment is a figment of your imagination.
Our perception is errant. Green is not inherent in the greenery.

Take a hard look at the indiscreet foliage.
Nature disregards Keats and Coleridge waxing lyrical,
while chlorophyll invites us to gaze on its detritus.
Should your interest in this stretch to Photosynthesis,
you'll realise plants require the ultraviolet and infrared,
leaving the green to be seen only in your head.

Green is a lie. A jump to conclusion.
A trick of the eye. An optical illusion.
By the look of it, you think you know a tree
until the prosaic curses the poetry.
And worse is - the spectral vision disperses.
Pedantic versus
Romantic verses.

Unconfirmed date

I'm not saying it's small as a pin
It's adequate, but awfully thin
She said 'God give me strength
There's no girth, it's all length –
But I'm willing to pencil you in'

Seldom asked questions

FAQ, FAQ, FAQ, FAQ, FAQ, FAQ, FAQ.
F. A. Q. - Right there at the back.
Frequently asked questions,
Frequently asked questions,
Just behind the trouble shooting section.
Every website, Every manual, Every second.
What's wrong with annual?

What's wrong with seldom asked questions
that no one's ever shared yet?
Bet it's better than repetitive fretting -
Are we there yet? Are we there yet? Are we there yet?

Where's the anomaly? The unusual investigation
into the out of the ordinary with no obvious explanation?
When is the rarely made enquiry?
Who seeks the unique mystery?
Where is that exceptional question mark that makes history?

Cross examined face to face or challenged on the phone. . .
'Where can I find the arrhythmic serenade of smokers
huddled in a rain beaten doorway hacking up phlegm . . .
as a ring tone?'

Seldom asked questions . . .

What does wildfire spread like?
Where exactly is a roundabout?
What's omnipresence all about?
Can you make a reservation without a doubt?

If literally is exact, and unique equals only ever one of –
How would you represent 'it's quite literally very unique'
as a fraction?

What is your favourite distance between two trees?

Out of Slate, Sleet, Slit, Slot, Slat, and Slut,
which is the most diagonal?

Seldom asked questions. . .

How come the film Never Ending Story finishes after 2 hours,
but Last of the summer wine goes on for fucking ever?

A hook shaped line of questioning
that leaves question marks attached.
Is it better to cover up a bruise,
or colour in the rest of your body maroon to match?

Seldom asked questions, bearing no suggestion of cliché,
but is a burnt saucepan at sunset what it all boils down to
at the end of the day?

The clue's in the title

His fingerprints are all over his fingers
His DNA matches his swab
There's a pubic hair that placed him there
At the crime scene surrounding his nob.

There's a video of him yelling
The evidence is compelling
He did the deed and spilt his seed
And it looks like an inside job.

Gravity be thy name

This immediately sounds odd,
Coming from an Atheist,
But it turns out, inexpediently
God does exist.

Not *the* god or *a* god or *your* god.
No, more like "Oh My Cognitive dissonance! –
Gravity's attraction has matched my resistance."

My god rocks, it ticks all the boxes.
It's what scientifically, undeniably, irrefutably, indisputably
Created the universe - in its entirety.
Every sun, every star, every planet and galaxy
And everything in it, and that includes you and me.
My god is gravity.

My god rocks, it ticks all the boxes.
Omnipresent, invisible, untouchable, intangible.
There's no enigma bigger or more magical.
You cannot smell it, you cannot hear it.
You can't reason why you cannot deny it,
But you'll always rely on its ubiquitous pull.
Without gravity we'd scatter away to infinity
And unravel into our constituent molecules.

My god stays grounded.
My god is cool.
The only rules are - that there aren't any rules
About evil and good. You do what you should
And you'll only live once with resultant exultance.

My god rocks, it ticks all the boxes.
Except for the one about squandering approximately
Most of your life thanking and praising
And praying and wailing and worshipping.
All that devotion and sacrifice.
All your life bowing, exalting and glorifying
And, even more terrifyingly absurd . . .
Spreading the word.

There's no one I abhor more
Than word spreaders on a mission to knock on my door.
Of all those responsible for waging war,
Top of my list is the evangelist.

So fuck off and go find a god of your own.
Some insecure psychopath sat on a throne,
All jealous and needy, won't leave you alone,
and relentlessly peeved at not being believed in.

My god wants for nothing,
Except to be known as the cause of creation,
The glue of the universal space-time continuum.
There's nothing here airy-fairy or mystical,
Superstitious or supernatural.
This god is seriously empirical.
So, lest you rather palaver with theory and claim,

Our father,
Who art in heavy.
Gravity be thy name.

Ten Haiku

Tipping point of view.
Perhaps fish say 'That's only
most of the iceberg.'

Every day I step
Way outside my comfort zone.
I get out of bed.

Blew up a balloon.
The girl who ran off with it
Took my breath away.

I can fart Mozart.
She said 'Smart – while you start that,
I'll queef in B flat'.

If Hugh Laurie ate
Jonathan Porrit, he'd be
Porrit Laurie ate.

Richard Dawkins shaped
Vibrator to cater for
Masturbatheists

Newspapers report
That love is more likely at
First sight than first thought.

Enough Viagra
To straighten up The Leaning
Tower of Pfizer

I laugh that only
Half of numbers can be halved.
God! - It's even odd!

Thought I'd bought a book
of baby names, but it was
full of adult names

Alan Wolfson twigging

There's no improvement

You make a three-legged-chair look like it's one leg short.
You make the things that I've stolen
feel like things that I've bought.
You squander your departures while you're planning to arrive.
You call the recently deceased the very recently alive.

You're neither speeding up nor slowing,
There's no improvement.
Still no improvement.

You've cancelled coming out by going,
There's no improvement.
Still no improvement.

You're wearing camouflage trousers, but your jacket's high viz.
You order a takeaway, and leave it where it is.
You flutter bunting up above a forecourt full of shit.
You scrape the sandwich filling out,
and make a sandwich out of it.

Your latest status keeps on showing
There's no improvement.
Still no improvement.

You're like a revolution without a movement.
There's no improvement.
Still no improvement.

19 upside down

Well looky here, I'm still around
I've not been shot, I didn't drown
I haven't been kicked to death by a clown
Or hooked up to a drip in my dressing gown

I didn't get iced by some cocaine grower
Or sliced up by a homicidal lawnmower
I haven't let a melanoma turn malignant brown
I'm in the pink, and I like to think I'm 19 upside down

The weird thing is – I've never felt more alive
Despite the sword of Damocles, and the reaper's scythe
And the likelihood that something important might snap
The next time I get up from my afternoon nap

They say youth is wasted on the young Maybe
breath is wasted on the lung
Girth is certainly wasted on the hung
And truth is wasted on the gung ho
I don't know though, I'm not on a go-slow, I'm going to a go-go
I've got a whole load of red paint to paint the town
I'm no shy teen, I'm 19 upside down

So lets twist again like we did last summer
Coz 61 is just another number
Is the glass half full? Is the glass half empty?
Am I over 60? Am I under twenty?
If you say I'm into 'decade seven', that's got an awful sound.
Whereas I'm far more comfortable agreeing to being 19 upside down

It has to be said when you stand on your head
It's not as easy to wine and dine
As it is calculating how I'll be celebrating on the day I turn 69.
So hoist me up by my ankles, and dangle me off the ground
Cos 61 is a lot more fun when you're 19 upside down

I'm a rebel

I am a rebel
I'm colouring in - I go over the lines
I just don't care
I ignore the signs and come in through the exit
Then, when no one expects it
I go out through the way in
I get away without paying or displaying
What I'm saying is I'm a rebel
I don't conform
Everyone's wearing their jeans torn at the knees
I keep my knees warm

I will walk on the grass
I wont hurry while stocks last
I'll ignore the front door when somebody knocks it
I jam three pin plugs into two pin sockets
My pocket's got a special pen holder . . . There's no pen in it
I ain't defending it
I just don't care

I tell you what gets my goat
When I'm watching a repeat and they say
'Don't vote - Lines are closed'
Well maybe I'm supposed to know that
But I do it anyway, and I pay -
So it only goes to show that
even though my call's belated -
I will not be dictated to

I feel most alive at the front of the queue
when the voice says counter number five please
I go straight to counter number two
And just wait there
Cos I'm a rebel

When the fasten seatbelt sign comes on
I take my seatbelt off
I pop handfuls of cough sweets when I don't have a cough
There's always a platform edge I'll stand too close to
I operate heavy machinery when I'm not supposed to
Like on Lemsip, 'cos I doubled the dose they recommended
I leave baggage at airports unattended

Cos I'm a rebel

I'll go online and give all my passwords away
I store lawn cuttings in my cutlery tray
And my shirts in fridges
I burn my bridges before I've crossed them
I'm searching for my keys - I haven't even lost them -
Cos they say they'll always be in the last place you look
Not me. When I find them, I hang them on the key hook
and carry on looking

Cos I'm a rebel

I refuse to rhyme with pebble, right?
I scream like a distorted guitar might
I won't go to Bethlehem in the direction of starlight

Oh, and one other thing -

I'm ambivalent about Marmite

Masochistic box of wasps blues

I'd stick my cock in a box of wasps
just to stop you from walking away.
I'd nail my scrotum to a totem pole,
if only you'd turn round and stay.

I'd shove a cactus up my arse
and ask you to never leave me.
If I did all that would you come on back
and rush me to A&E.

They say don't you go beating yourself up, but it's my way of getting through it.
They say don't you go torturing yourself, but hey, who else is going to do it?

If I jam my bollocks in a workbench vice,
would you wind it up tight and lock it?
If I fasten my nips to crocodile clips,
would you plug me in a power socket?

If I clamped your teeth around my urethra,
could we go back to the way it's been?
And If I smeared my cock with Novichok,
would you visit me in quarantine?

They say don't you go beating yourself up, but it's my way of getting through it.
They say don't you go torturing yourself, but hey, who else is going to do it?

If I Baked my todger in a Jammy dodger,
would you come back and have it for tea?
If I'd series linked a box set of my sphincter
would you watch it on the sofa with me?

If I l smeared myself in gefilte fish
and let you feed me to Vanessa Feltz,
would you keep me chained up in a cage in your room
while you fucked off and lived somewhere else?

Wales boasts the world's largest concentration of sharp corners.
The edges of this very page first met at right angles in Angelsea.
However, the Welsh Male Voice Choir that accompanies this poem (deluxe edition only)
is neither sharp nor flat

Sharp corners come from Wales

Honey comes from bumble bee porn
Ripples come from tiny tears being torn
Parallel lines come from finger nails
And sharp corners come from Wales

Solidarity comes from Polish builders
Decadence comes from lily gilders
Container-ship comes between the docks and the jails
And sharp corners come from Wales

Lachrymose samosas you could slash your wrists with
Are stored in a maternity ward in Aberystwyth
Where East European maestros have their priceless instruments
Brought by liveried minions to the delivery room
To be tuned to a baby's cry
The Welsh are all born singing Mae hen wlad fy nhadau*

Frigidaire and Hotpoint come from heat exchangers
Alien abductions come from incomplete strangers
Trains of thought come off the rails
And sharp corners come from Wales

**pronounced My hen lard vun add eye*

The Dalai Lama's quiff

My therapist alleges
there's a boating lake she dredges
in pursuit of bevelled edges,
but in truth the level best of them
are not forgotten at the bottom,
but living in the contoured hedges
that all adorn the sculpted frills
around the lawns of Beverly Hills.

The need to find 'soft angles' leaves
us hunting in Los Angeles,
where arcing Art Nouveau is fine,
but there's no wavy line as pissed as
separates the Beverly Sisters.

Be that as it maybe, but allegedly
the greatest bevelled edge'd be
the one that's often found around Nepal.
The smoothest pointlessness of all -
Upon the crown of one who revels
in the swivels of a swell fixed up with gel
so soft and swish, it looks as if
the competition's looking stiff -
compared to The Dalai Lamas quiff.

Benefit fraud

Lies the size of the side of a bus
Benefit fraud shored up on a corrupt abacus
Witness the perjurers urging us to quit -
Muckle Gove, Bogus Johnson, and Iain Dunking Shit

They call me the Mars rover *(12 bar blues)*

They call me The Mars Rover,
And I'm gonna rove all over you.
Yeah they call me The Mars Rover,
And I'm gonna rove all over you.
I've got an Alpha Particle X-Ray Spectrometer
to monitor what's what, and who's who.

As long as the sun's glowing,
I can keep going with my solar battery pack.
I got this God given gift
to kvetch, shtup and sift the nutty slack.
I'll have armfuls of samples
and some curious looking item
when I come back.

I go poking round the crust.
I go rolling in the dust.
Yeah it's bleak n harsh n rough,
But I got Martian wanderlust ..

Yeah they call me The Mars Rover,
And I'm gonna rove all over you.
I've got a load of CCTV things
So you can see things from a Martian point of view.

Isolation is a perk, in fact I prefer working on my own.
You can see me on a TV screen,
But you can't reach me on the phone.
I'm no remote control patsy,
I'm just glad the paparazzi leave me alone.

They call me The Mars Rover,
I'm kinda red all over monochrome.
It's colder than the tundra
3 hundred million miles away from home.
I wasn't born to run, or born slippy, or born to be wild . . .
I was born to roam.

Licences

Tuesday morning I come to my senses.
I go down to the office that allocates licences.
I say 'I need a licence'.

The lady behind the counter reaches down to fetch a
locked box from under a shelf.
She re-emerges, adjusts herself,
removes the lid and urges me to consider its contents.
She says 'Which one do you want?'
I say 'Show me one that says 'Licence' in a nice
sans serif font'.

I sense a little tension.
Then she says
'I've got a pilot's licence,
a pirate's licence,
a wireless licence,
an ultra violet licence,
a licence to suffer in silence,
a licence to suffer in Spanish,
a licence to vanish,
a licence to varnish,
a licence to harness the energy of a toddler's tantrum to power
your car.
A licence to marry,
a licence to carry on as you are.
A licence to carry on as your mum,
a licence to fart out your bum,
a licence to start a religion,
a licence to startle a pigeon,
a licence to show the film Bridge on the River Kwai,
a licence to drop a fridge on Jamiroquai,
a licence to buy a telly,
a licence to fly a helicopter. . . .'

I stopped her right there.
I said 'What I would like is a licence to do
anything I care to.
A nice an' simple licence that lets me do approximately What I like,
When I like,
How I like,
Where I like,
With whom I like.
Assume I like the merchandise,
I'll make it worth it if it fits'.

She looks me in the eyes and says 'This is
licences.
You want birth certificates'.

Hemispheres

It's forever midnight somewhere
on the other side of noon.
There's a place in space with your back to the sun
where it's constantly full moon.
It's a lyrical dichotomy
that waxes yang and yin.
While you're contemplating Autumn,
Someone's celebrating Spring.

Cole Porterloo

To the tune of 'Every time we say goodbye'

Every time we screw, before I'm through
I have to pee a little
Soon as I've come, I'm on the run
To the lavatory to piddle

When love has ended, we should both curl up in a ball
But my bladders distended, and I hear the porcelain call

Every time we fuck, it's just my luck
I have to piss a little
That après shag, Light up a fag,
That's what I miss a little

Just one more sign of maturing
But how strange the change from semen to urine

Every time we meet – make it en-suite

Like being there

Those Glastonbury tickets sold out in record time.
And I'm a bit too late booking my festival escape.
But then we get told the whole world is on hold and nobody goes.
To be honest, it was hard to avoid a
sliver of schadenfreude.
Now we'll all have to make do with
watching old ones on the telly.
For authenticity, I'll still be wearing my wellies
and clutching a soggy pancake of spicy veg.

Then, Starting from the edge,
I'll cover my TV with masking tape,
until nothing can be seen
except for a tiny post-it note size shape
in the middle of the screen.
And I'll turn the volume up loud
as vintage moments are shown,
so it feels like I'm actually there in the crowd,
filming it all on my phone.

Zagreb

I arrived alongside the edge of Zagreb
And tried to buy an A to Zed
In the shop at a Croatian petrol station.
But they only had a Zed to A.
They said Zagreb is spelt that way.

Crete

I ditched solid city environment
for a soft sunny beach they've got on Crete.
I prefer my sand without cement.
I'm pro Crete, I'm not con Crete.

Totnes

Despite the fact that
erratic attics with casements outnumber basements,
Totnes is not necessarily
less cellary than loftness.

If Poets made movies ....
Poetry themed Film and TV remakes

Monty Python's Life Of Byron

Shelley Tubbies

The Good, The Bad, and The Hegley

Duffy The Vampire Slayer

The Full Brontë

Mama Maya.

Yeats on a plane

The Big Bukowski

Plath to Glory

Get Goethe

The 40 year old Virgil

Frost Gump

The Great British Berkoff

Coleridge on the river Kwai

Point Blake

Pulp Dickinson

Tennyson Waltz.

Motion's Eleven.

Honey I shrunk the Keats.

50 Shades of Graves

Tourists

They come over here
with their legs and their thoughts
and their digestive systems
and sensible shorts

They walk on our pavements
and look at our trees
They soak up our sunshine
and welcome our breeze

They come over here
absorbing the light
Considering things -
It just isn't right

Look - there's one over there
in my line of sight -
obscuring my view with
their width and their height
Typical tourists! You'll always find them
preventing you seeing whatever's behind them.

They come over here from away over there
Taking up room and displacing our air
Look how carefree they seem with their breadth and their scope
and their sense of adventure, and vigour, and hope

And they see our sights and they fill their hearts
They're not like us. They're not 'from around these parts'
Their memories are fond and the sun always shone
But it's grim and it's wan once the tourists have gone

The darkest serendipity

The photographer and the choreographer
Are frozen in flight in black and white.
The arsonist and the ventriloquist
Swap incendiary tips without moving their lips.
Frilly ladies in frocks crook their fingers like cocks
As they giggle their heavenly sip of tea.
Suddenly, Crack! - Collision
Then howls of derision.
It is the darkest serendipity.

Of all the cars parked outside all the bedrooms
of all the motels off all the highways
on all the outskirts of all the towns
in all the world . . .
She had to reverse into mine.

The Press are busy tailing a dizzy red head in a red dress,
When the prang in the parking bay sends the feral gang my way.
The arsonist sparks a panic,
The choreographer splits,
The photographer shoots off,
The ventriloquist gottles out,
And I'm left flanked by the fragrant frocks of
The Vague Ladies Society.
They suspect an awkward scene and disperse,
Surgically stretched away in a stretched limousine.
Or was it a hearse?

I feel the fool in me awake.
The reel and the take up spool begin to wind
As I fill up with the movie she left behind in my head.
We explored most of our leading roles in bed,
Where inquisitive young lovers easily uncover more tiny
Journeys of discovery,
Than they do swerving up precarious learning curves.

She gets out of the car. Observes.
Examines the scar, shouts fuck five times,
Looks up and finds my face.
She makes out she can't place me.
Then she can.
She sucks in another softly spoken 'fuck'
as she walks towards me from her pimped up van.
"Hey man, still clumsy after all these years." She purrs,
sashaying past the paparazzi.
I threw her a look that looked like like a knife.
"Back into my car. Back into my life?"
She sidled up with her 'diddums' bluff
and her eyebrow knitting stuff.
I said "that's far enough.
On a mission – or just fishin'?"
She notes the suspicion,
slides her hand up inside my vest and,
with her lips pressed close, she whispers
"Yeah - it's a mystery.
Let's get to work on my apology"

We had bags of history
And satchels of biology.
Turned out to be the darkest serendipity.

Low definition omnibus edition

Top deck.
Front seat.
Last bus.
Cold and heat.
Heat and cold team up to
steam up the window
that ends up all rendered
diffused and translucent.
The view is a nuisance of condensation
droplets on glaze in a haze of temptation.
Breath's manifest microscopic beads urging
that its pristine matrix needs disturbing.

This irresistible misty canvas
stands tantalisingly near,
Demanding to be marred.
Pleading to be smeared.
Testing your resistance.
Insisting you foist your
Opening daub across the moisture.

And there you sit right in front of it.
So you curve a slit with your finger tip
And watch the wet wound weep and drip.
Acid lemon sodium street lamps
And their entourage of orange filaments
Leak their bendy running brilliance
Along the arc of your transparent mark.

And the scar bleeds descending wet tentacles
That trickle fast to the bottom of the glass
and pool along the black rubber seal.
Rivulets meander and gang up to reveal
an illuminated streetscape escaping
through the liquid scribbled window.

Hazy blurred lamp lights
Halos round tail lights
Rainbows round headlights
Silhouettes against the oncoming bright night.
Another double decker window,
half a bus high and flush alongside,
passes right beside you.
Somebody catches sight
of your warm cream and white
cabin scattered with passengers
watching them watching you watching them.
Glancing through demystified patches of steam
before gliding off unseen to where you've just been.
It's a bus window movie screen
showing the coming and going.
Cinéma vérité, low definition.
The omnibus edition

Stars over London

Don't you think a twinkle in the dark'll sparkle brighter right above The Tate?
When the dirt in certain contributions to pollution starts to dissipate,
Let's participate . . .

You'll be wishin' fuel emission quite disappears.
The night's crystal clear as diamond sharpness in the darkness.

Suddenly, I can see Stars over London.
That's Mars over London - shining bright as Zippo lighters.

Heaven knows the population never knows there's constellations
hiding above them,
But slide that thing undone,
and the Milky Way will pour down over London

If your thing's Celestial bling, behold chandelearrings!
That's heaven revealing - The Zodiac is overacting.

Suddenly, I can see Stars over London.
That's Mars over London - shining bright as Zippo lighters.

Particles will permanently mask the mighty firmament
Behind the pollution. We've found a solution,
For a scintillating stellar revolution.

Lumps of granite, Stars and planets winking above us,
linking up lovers.
Loose the text and use a sextant.

Suddenly, I can see Stars over London.
That's Mars over London - shining bright as Zippo lighters.

Shooting stars and satellites
Are lost to cars and traffic light-Beams up from the city.
It seems such a pity,
Those motorists don't notice it's so pretty.

Suddenly, I can see Stars over London.
That's Mars over London - shining bright as Zippo lighters.

Missing you is hitting me

The distance between us is the length of lightening
We've past critical torque, still the connection's tightening
Until hairline fractures fail and cracks form gaps
That let the light inside
So suddenly It dawns on me
The obvious is blindingly

Missing you is hitting me
Like miseryflexology
This emptiness is filling me
The overspilling's killing me
The worst thing is I'm bursting with
The pressure building up inside me
Still it pours impossibly
More nothing than can fit in me

Missing you is hitting me
Like bolts of electricity
Exploding for alternity
Enough to power a whole city tower block apartment
Chock full of lovers not meant to be apart
Longing to be a part of each other's heart.
You see Missing you is hitting me
So near, so far be it for me
To stay on target if
I'm positive I'm negative
My aim is indiscreetly skew
I'm missing you

Placebo

'I need a placebo' I screamed at the Quack.
'According to Google
my hypochondria's back.'
The Doctor unlocked a box of tricks and enquired,
'Are you tired of being sick or are you sick of being tired?'

'Quick - Invent some affliction, make me pee in a cup -
C'mon where's my prescription? '

'I'm making it up'.

She gave me a bottle,
there was nothing in it.
She said 'Take one of these invisible pills every minute'.

Then she insists there's specific directions to follow
But a little pill that isn't there's a little hard to swallow.
I said 'What if there are side effects
and I get into feeling fine?'
She said 'Begin to double up the dose
and you'll hardly have the time'.

She took my temperature, my pulse,
and my dignity and then
she said 'Have you had this before?
Well you've got it again'.

'You're just a mocked up imposter, you're not a proper Doc
So don't jive me none of that Post hoc ergo propter hoc.'

'Those are classic symptoms, It's gibberish you've got -
You'll always catch gobbledegook whenever you Google De doc'.

Then she took out a chisel and a Black & Decker
and was about to operate, but I suddenly felt better.

Deadline

Ice and snow turn twice as slow as the slow hand of a clock.
Standing on top of the North pole, the whole of me revolves about my core
once - every twenty four hours.

Meanwhile, halfway to the southernmost,
another post of me rotates upon the equator
at greater than the speed of sound.
Over a thousand miles an hour, spinning around
the girth of the Earth.

Distance is worthless.
Time stops, and time flies past as fast as light.
Time is killed. Doesn't put up much of a fight.
The two of me are standing still, and there we stay
moving neither closer nor further away.
Tropical and Polar. Baked to a crisp and Frozen stiff.

There's a cliff edge racing towards my feet
And a curbstone rising up to meet my face.
I'm hurtling aimlessly through space, anticipating the point of an arrow.
Reach and range are drawing in short and narrow.
Craving collapses, so easily crushed as it rushes into
the black hole of I hope so.

My slow rocketing won't stop a contradiction.
The doctor's contract is shrinking,
The shrink is contracting.
These citizens are acting like the
The Champions of Ambient Complicity.
Bricks and humming electricity.
Hissing gas and pissing water.
Minimal isn't less is mortar.
Send me a lifeline. Extend me a deadline.
The dead line-up on the other side of us.
The deadline's up. It was only a matter of time.

Twelve elevenths of an hour

I was locked in a room
With nothing at all,
Apart from a clock on the wall.
Just a regular clock.
It wasn't fast, it wasn't small.
It wasn't slow, it wasn't large.
It could neither be described as above or below average.
There was nothing about it to shout,
Or write home, or a poem about.
I thought for a moment
It might lack means of support and ought to fall down,
But it didn't.
Its fixings were hidden at the back,
so it just hung around,
parked up a wall,
unremarkable after all,
and standard as bog.
It wasn't even digital, it was analogue.

And there wasn't a sound in my prison
Except for the rhythm of the battery driven mechanism
of the clock.
And I'd rock with the tock,
and glaze over as I fixed my gaze on the hands
that pretended to stand perfectly still
Whilst slightly, secretly, circling, until
I had reckoned, one hour five minutes and 27 seconds
Would pass between the next time the big and little hands cross,
and the last.

Or more accurately, 65 minutes 27 and a quarter seconds elapse each time
the minute hand laps the hour hand.
Which happens to be 12 elevenths of an hour –
That is, the length of the interval to which I was referring,
As a fraction, is exactly 65.454545454545454545 recurring.

So I sat hands on lap
watching hands overlapping.
I was trapped in detention, did I mention that?
And all because I was watching the clock
and not paying attention to the lesson being taught,
so they taught me a lesson:

Time really drags when you watch it.
So watch it – and don't get caught.

Changing cubicle

Despite the sign that read 'Stop! Changing Cubicle'
I was sceptical as I stepped inside the receptacle
and pulled closed the pretty curtain.
I was pretty certain that when I stepped out,
I was somebody else in an entirely different shop.
This was highly disconcerting.
So I left my suspicions in the air conditioning
and walked back onto the street
where I immediately melted in the heat.
I discreetly morphed into an amorphous cloud of vapour
with a paper receipt, and then evaporated completely.
Above the lofts I wafted towards the ventilator which
serviced that very changing booth, and surfaced later
as a variation of the truth.
Like a fool drowning, I cooled down in a tin duct.
I got sucked into a conduit. I got conned, which I admit,
to my surprise, I'd been had.
And they didn't even have me in my size.

Fear of missing out

I'm overwhelmed with F.O.M.O.
It's hard to kick. I'm sick. I'm Mophobic.
I'd go out to a show though, but there's a list to go over,
So I'm flapping about like a windswept comb-over.

My schedule is listing under the weight of listings
My modus is to vacillate my way to miss things,
I'm intent on events, but prevented by FOMO
I've got six hot tickets, and a flyer for Shlomo.

There's a forward planning party, there's a retrospective,
There's the chronic inability to be selective.
There's a slam, there's burlesque, there's a gig in Inverness,
Seen the preview, heard the promo,
But my style is cramped by FOMO.

I'm stymied by Mophobia.
No wine and dine, and no beer.
I'm caught at home here, can't go outside,
like a rabbit in the headlines of the What's On Guide
'cause I know your bash is bound to clash -
Should I stay or should I go, dear?

Penzance crime wave

It's been several days since I came back from Penzance
But despite a good rinse, there's still sand in my pants.
And the aroma of fish, and the taste of salt -
It's not my fault - I got assaulted
by a gang of mermaids.

The police recently staged a series of dawn raids
to stop that sort of thing.
When the tide went out, the police moved in,
Hiding behind their camouflage of kelp,
But it didn't help.
Neither did sea CCTV.

This is what happened to me.
On the beach, each mermaid laid in wait.
I sat alone licking a ninety nine, when off went the ring tone on my phone.
That's when they snuck up behind me and spiked my cone.
I ate a bit more, and then about a second later
me and my ice cream were flaked out on the floor.

They dragged me down to the bottom of the bay
and had their wicked fishy way with me.
I tried to resist but I couldn't.
Relentlessly they kissed me with their fishy kisses.
They wouldn't stop.
They foisted their moistened womanly fins and scales upon me;
honestly, those slippery slapper flappy fishy females
were really quite sadistic.
What a way to behave.
Now I'm just another statistic in the rising mermaid crime wave.
Levels are up
but the tide is turning

Guns in the world jam

Barack Obama said 'Yes we can'
I say - What if all the guns in the world jam?
No one shoot nobody because nobody can

What if all the knives in the world fold?
You'll cut your own fingers and you're grip'll lose hold
Gonna drop the knife
Gonna save a life
Nobody gets stabbed and we all live to grow old

What if all the bombs in the world fail to detonate? – *yeah yeah yeah*
Wouldn't it be great – *yeah yeah yeah*

What if all the world was satisfied?
Nobody run and nobody hide
'cause nobody would need to
all our differences agreed to
And all the armies in the world decide to take a break.

Forever.

We'll have nothing to fear but the weather . . .
Er - and the earthquake . . .
And the meteorite . . .
And disease and blight . . . .
And the parasite
And green kryptonite
But that's all right
Cause all the money from the fighting sitting in a pot
That's a shit load o money since the fighting stopped
And all you got to do is fetch it
Re-direct it so the wretched are protected
And the poor have-nots will now have got
Hot food on their plate – *yeah yeah yeah*
Wouldn't that be great – *yeah yeah yeah*

Everybody congregate in the open air,
And what we do there is dance and sing
And frolic about and and do our thing
Underneath the sky, and I tell you why –
Coz love is love and not fade or die
And all that hate will evaporate
Wouldn't that be great – *yeah yeah yeah*
Wouldn't that be great – *yeah yeah yeah*

Give your tail a wag, Get your blues all healed
Go to sleep in a bag, And wake up in a field
Tumble out of the bars With all your secrets revealed
Slumber under the stars And wake up in a field

There's a rock n roll band kicking open the sky
Everybody's getting down, getting up, getting high
Right in front of the stage the mosh is turning contagious
(There's a piss-head in the distance having need of some assistance)

There are fairies, there's a carnival, there's drumming and dance
You can fall in love or fall in mud or give peace a chance
When you witnessed what the moon did
for the wasted and the wounded
All you tasted was a feeling for the power of sexual healing

Give your tail a wag, get your blues all healed
Go to sleep in a bag, and wake up in a field
Tumble out of the bars with all your secrets revealed
Slumber under the stars and wake up in a field

What if all the guns in the world jam?

I'm out of here

I'm unwinding a coil,
I'm untying a knot
I'm puncturing a hermetically sealed pot
I'm sliding out from under a log
Releasing the pressure, escaping the smog
to where the air is fresher. Have you heard the news?
I'm pleasing myself, I'm easing out of tight shoes

I'm leaving this pig poke, I'm saving my bacon
You think it's a big joke, I'm busy escaping -
(Contingent upon dodging flecks of spittle).
This arena's been a little too astringent and brittle

Now I'm shifting co-ordinates, I'm moving the axes
I'm tearing the map up, unravelling tapestries.
I'm cauterising this thing that disables
And atrophies. And numbs. And cripples
I'm disconnecting the jumper lead cables
And removing the alligator clips from my nipples

The cut is reluctant, the sever severe
I'm not scared any more.
Like before – I couldn't run out of fear
Now I've run out of fear,
I'm out of here

My girlfriend is a zombie

Her cappuccino machine is a deluxe De'Longhi
Her central heating boiler is a Potterton combie
She wears American Apparel and Abercromby
But, on the minus side, I cannot hide
the fact my girlfriend is a zombie.

When ever she speaks, she'll utter a growl
Her pelvis creaks like a guttural vowel
She's not very together, it has to be said
She's falling apart, but she's not quite dead

Her eyes are glazed, her face is white
She only ever comes out at night
she'll wander into a club in a trance
but the trouble starts when she tries to dance
cos when she flings her arms out – her arms keep on going,
so there's all that retrieving and gluing and sewing.
Can't tell what direction her limbs'll fly off in
luckily she's got spare ones back home in her coffin.

She's been an extra in Thriller, The wife of Attila
and a cushion on Peter Cushing's bed
She got muffy with Buffy, and sawn off with Shaun of the
Dawn of the night of the living dead

My girlfriend is a Zombie, I can't reach her on the phone
Apparently the signal's weak deep in the twilight zone
But round about the midnight hour, when I think she's slept enough
I tie a message to a bat, and let it home in on her chuff.

Yes, you shout 'Outrageous!' Those creatures are contagious
You know she's gonna pounce on you and kill you in your bed.
And yet . . . as I'm about to arrive I've never felt more alive
than with a flesh-eating zombie giving me head.

Decanter fantasy

A lot of people know that
whenever the level of the terracotta sugar bowl runs low
we top it up.
Although few appreciate the anguish in doing so as sugar
left below is doomed to languish
forever parked along the bottom.
Abandoned and unused, past its best,
depressed, all in the dark and forgotten.
And understandably miffed, each time we lift the lid.
Just as it glimpses daylight, and brightens with the anticipation of realising
its life's purpose,
a refill of fresh grains renders it surplus to requirements,
and there it remains, trapped in endless retirement.
So close to fulfilling its ambition,
its calling, its mission, its dolce vita,
its destiny to make tea sweeter,
its raison d'etre. Etcetera.

Blocked in the bottom of the bowl, kept on hold.
Smothered, neglected, uncollected.
Escape - always a scoop away. One tiny tantalising teaspoon between
keeping covered and the sweet taste of freedom.
It must come soon. Surely the sugar's earned its turn to be
ferried from bowl to cup, but alas no.
Like pressed snow beneath fresh snow, it gets buried.
It gets topped up.
The interminable wait it clocked up bears not a grain of leverage
on its claim to assimilate with a hot beverage.

The lid goes back, its hopes are dashed.
It won't get splashed or stirred, or get involved,
or dissolve into teas of joy.

It won't be heard, or touched, or its sweetness tasted.
No more will it be seen,
except for seeing its potential being wasted.
The very basis of this wretched echelon is fated to be put upon,
and left unconsummated,

So hold on, wait a while and behold
another disappearance beneath a greater pile of Tate & Lyle, while caked
and stale old stained sugar
is left unloved and fallow.
Is this a shallow cover up?
Low level interference?
Or more likely an anthropomorphic trite decanter fantasy?

Link responsibly

Cuddle with caution

And hug in proportion

Emerge with precaution

As Alan does.

I doubt dates and mock myths

Like love laughs at locksmiths

And Covid cackles at calendars

(Playing Scrabble, I tried to add the letters LO to the word VENTRILOLQUIST. It was pointed out that such a word does not exist anywhere, So as consolation, I claimed the word for myself, and wrote this by way of a definition.)

The Loventriloquist

She probably inhabits an elusive coven
The Loventriloquist
She'll have you kissed sweetly without moving her lips
She'll undress you completely
You'll strip, you'll confess.
You'll crack in a way you would never have guessed from that imperceptible twist of her hips.
You may arch backward, straining to lean away,
But The Loventriloquist is holding sway
And you're folding her way.

You capitulate.
You're manipulated.
You never suspected you're so susceptible to projection.
She escapes detection at the very moment
She captures your affection
And enrols you and controls you
And makes you say whatever you're told to. She'll insist. She'll flex her wrist.
She'll say "Who's the mummy?"
The Loventriloquist, dummy.

You're convinced in an instant.
Unconsciously watching her send another order to surrender.
You're being driven
The frozen grin you're given
Is only there for putting words in,
Or taking them out, according to her whim.
Your jaw will open or close at her bidding.
Her winning ways grow as you're willpower loses,
You'll say whatever The Loventriloquist chooses.

Your weakness amuses her.
Chances and clues were there – all of them missed.
You just couldn't resist.
You had no choice.
You lost your voice.
Your heart is spoken for.
You can't ignore The Loventriloquist
For this will surely come to pass -
Your mouth will manically gape and shut mechanically
when she sticks her right hand right up your arse
and makes a fist,
The Loventriloquist.

WTF just happened?

It was an interminable Tuesday
a tediously slow news day
with incidents of note a little sparse,
save for rival religious zealots,
like ballistic Anusol pellets,
persistently getting up each others arse

Suddenly, there was a blinding light and deafening thunder
The heavens above were torn asunder
and The Good Lord God appeared – a little pissed.

He said "You believers are all done.
It's the Atheists who've won -
There is no 'Holy One'. I don't exist"

Then he pulled out a spliff. Took a toke,
and with that disappeared in a puff of smoke.

Up Brexit Creek

It's time we had an English war
With swords and shields and fields and flags
With floral crocheted pockets of resistance
And Laura Ashley body bags

We can turn a fracas into a skirmish
We'll furnish the troops with gardening shears
What they do to their knackers is not for the squirmish
A scythe up the caboose can reduce you to tears

Moustachioed generals with beetroot faces
Retreating hairlines and advancing dementia,
'We'd send reinforcements, but they lost all their cases
At Calais' terminal world of adventure'

We climb in our dinghies, all slapstick and splashing,
Drop our paddles in the shit in a fit of pique
And we'll give Johnny Foreigner a damn good thrashing
For leaving us marooned up Brexit Creek

Slip sliding away

Instead of going shopping,
I decided to go sliding in the snow.
I led my sled to this slope I know and slid down as fast as I could,
But couldn't cope with the stopping,
and ended upside-down in the cold.
In that tiny moment of fun
I was nine years old, whereas in fact I'm 71.
And now there's nothing for supper.

12th night

Take your decorations down.
Pack your knees up Mother Brown.
Pile the trees up out of town
inside the designated zone.
Or burn the desiccated lonely needles,
clinging needlessly, senseless, ornament-less and un-spruced.
Turn your timetable back to what you're used to.
Halt the ringing, stop the singing,
and colour in the silent night with irony.
Violent night.
Howly night,
all ambulance and police car sireny.
That joy and revelry is but a memory.
A Christmas shaped bruise that'll fade by February.

And then - one evening in the middle of summer,
by the edge of a cabinet, by chance you'll discover
an obstinate inch or two of tinsel
trapped on the wall by a brass drawing pin
still thumbed in tight and determined to remain.
The gauche of Christmas past, stubborn as a stain.

And a shiver will lay claim
to where the warmth went missing while
you were reminiscing.
And the nights will draw in,
and the days will shorten,
and suddenly Autumn has turned into Winter.
Silhouettes of blue veined trees begin t' freeze
against the milk wash sky.
The seasons fly by and their brilliance palls. Enlist
resilience. Deck the halls.

Audi the destroyer

Every day a spider spins a most graceful web between
the hedge and my car,
and dew drops attach superfluous decoration to the design
like opulent promenade illuminations . . .
and every day I drive away to see this
diaphanous chandelier collapse into a pitiful string, wafting
derelict in the breeze.

The spider is neither the least bit discouraged nor edified.
It blissfully ignores the fundamental flaw
in the hedge/web/car triumvirate,
and labours through the night at its misguided construct
with fastidious futility.

Next day there's another gossamer doily
confidently secured to the driver's door,
cunningly positioned exactly where the last one hung
just before it was rent asunder.
Again I drive off reluctantly, to see the filigree silk fail,
and hang limp and forlorn as Crystal Palace in ruins.

This has been going on for weeks.
Now each morning I bid farewell to my deluded little pal
and drive away pondering the pointlessness
that betrays meticulous endeavour, and how it is
that one can create the most delicate beauty ever to behold,
and still be a bit thick.

Hats

A lot of poets step up to the plate
and talk about all the things that they hate.
Now I hate that.

Something else I hate is wearing a hat. Indoors.

Some people do, and some people don't care.
Some people will, and some people won't wear a hat indoors.
It can cause disapproval and calls for its removal.
Or more likely invite little ripples of applause.
On the other hand you might be ambivalent about the indoor titfer,
After all, let's face it - everyone's wearing one at a Barmitzvah.

But, people are starting rumours, cos they see me and assume as
how I've always got a hat to put my head in,
It's OK to go round spreading that I'm obviously dreading
putting my bald head on display. No way!
I love my head this way – all smooth and hairless.
Call me baldy if you like, I couldn't care less.
In truth Hirsute never suited me.

You can see your reflection on my spherical crest.
And ladies, sex with a slap-head is the best.
Cos when WE go down on furry town – unlike hairy men,
There's something for you to doodle on with a felt tip pen.

Yes, it sounds astounding -
If I love my shiny bonce,
How come I'm always found in
fancy hats to ponce around in.
Well, it's not to keep my bald head hidden in a sheath.
No, it's to cover up the embarrassing tiny little hat
I'm wearing underneath.

(Removes hat to reveal smaller hat perched within)

HAPPY NOW?

The shopping precinct turned bleak inside,
fell unconscious for weeks.
Then it coughed up a trickle of piss and died.

Now ruthless white sunlight silently scorches the corpse.
And having baked and bleached and dried
the last of the stubborn damp rain streaked romance
from the dirt clogged paving slabs,
it drains the remaining colour from the afternoon,
leaving anaemic bed sheet sized torn advertising posters clinging to hoardings. Giant grinning faces.
Ultra violet faded dirty turquoise grey arms and hands proffer obsolete stuff.

Hundreds of dust encrusted flagstones of two shades,
bacon pink or bacon fat, are scattered about the piazza
with that disregard for design consideration and aesthetic sensibility
we like to call 'Municipal abstract'.

Devoid of pedestrian eyes, unavoidable walkways stretch
unnecessarily wide and pale and vacant
between shut up shops,
and boarded up bookmakers,
and yesterday's newsagents.

Ornamental litter is caught in corners, the rest in little crevices.
But old local newspapers, paralysed flat and airless,
refuse to dance the tumble weed
or even levitate a quiet dying breath.
Deformed pages creased open expose
grim photographs of identical terraced houses up for sale,
each labelled with a price tag and an apology.

Property in sorry state
Premises in need of decoration.
In need of renovation.
In need of modernising.

In need of sterilising.
In need of demolition.

The sun beats the paper shiny,
and yellows the ancient newsprint brittle.
Next to the abandoned property section, cheap clutter and
components of no purpose or value fill the classified columns,
along with grease stains, and coffee stains,
and discreet mature blondes offering immature euphemisms
'all night long'.

A thoughtless patchwork of grubby signs are preaching to the deserted
Mismatched in drab council livery or clumsy gloss paint,
they appear to prohibit everything.
No hawkers, Licensed stallholders only
Do not smoke in doorways.
No more than 2 school children in hallways,
Never stand on tables, always read the labels . . .

Overweight metal plates and forbidding plaques yell at nobody
in brutal block capitals

NO BALL GAMES, NO CLIMBING
NO BUSKERS, NO MIMING
NO ROLLER SKATES, SPITTING
NO CYCLING, NO KNITTING
NO BREAKDANCING, SKATEBOARDS,
NO HOPPING, NO SKIPPING
IF YOU'RE FOUND COMMITTING
A BREACH OF THE PEACE
OR HITTING A POLICEMAN, OR LOOKING OBESE . . .

The constraints never cease . . .
But beneath them, sprayed in silver grey,
a fat meaty question mark is tagged at the end of the graffiti that reads

HAPPY NOW?

Lavernock

When I was a boy
I sat on the beach at Lavernock
and cracked open a pebble so I could watch
the first daylight in a billion years
dazzle and blind the rough divide
that last witnessed beams of a younger sun
that shone before mankind was born.
Then I rejoined the fractured counterparts along
their perfect match, closing the scathed fissure to a hairline,
squeezing out the light, capturing the shock and brevity
of the moment.

When I grew up, my heart was dashed.
It broke apart, and the sadness of a millennium
flooded into the split, rendering it
beyond repair.
So I threw it away and grew a new one there.
Smooth and round and flat and bevelled,
and perfectly balanced and comfortably held.
Waiting for you to come along
And spin it and skim it across the sea
And with every splash
my heart would bounce and sing with glee.

Upney

I've lived round here for many a year
Never knowing it existed
I'm really crap at scrutinising a map
So It's hardly surprising I'd missed it

But if you look for a sign down the district line -
In amongst threats to trespass and parking,
There's a daft little station with no known location
Just opposite apposite Barking

Upney. That's right Upney – not Putney, or Chutney
or Hackney or Hockney. No – Upney.
It's not even a tuppenny ha'ppenny town
It's just a name on a plate that makes the train wait
Neither going Upney down

The bit that's called Upney ends rather abruptly
at the boundary line of the station.
It's bound to be found to be more en route
than a bona fide destination

Once a platform concerto featured Astrud Gilberto,
who sang of a Brazilian dreamer.
She was tall, and tanned, and young, and lovely,
The girl from Up-ney-ma

So I'm thinking what if John Lloyd's 'Meaning of Liff '
were to give this name some function
I think it would look better off in his book
than hanging about up the junction'

Upney: A highly contagious involuntary reflex leg spasm thought to be responsible for the great Can Can epidemic of 1832, the original cause of which has been traced all the way back to Mother Brown.

Squeaky Stan

He doesn't much care for a joke.
When asked for his favourite one liner,
He pulled a face like a ripped bin liner, and said 'Coke'.
And then the bloke who asked got his legs broke.

Squeaky Stan is a volatile man, and he looks like a tramp.
He's as highly strung as a cocked trebuchet,
and mad as piranha in a lava lamp.

The once blonde tuft atop his bulging sack of a head,
is now a depleted greasy gobbet of nicotine and lemon curd.
Beneath it swivel lopsided yellow eyes
wedged into a leather-beaten face,
like two beads of undigested sweetcorn peering out of a turd.

It's the sound of his own girly voice that incenses him.
He'll posture and grimace to appear more menacing,
but it comes out - if anything - a little bit camp.
So he boils up in silence, and bursts into violence.

He won't eat a fried egg unless there's a
cigarette stubbed out in it,
still jammed in the lips of the cook who served it,
who looked unappealing, and so needed 'dealing with'
Because 'He deserved it'.
(His musical taste is awfully dull
but he loves the percussion of skillet on skull.)

He killed his mum just for bringing him chewing gum that wasn't
the one with the picture of Harry Potter.
So he shot her.
Then of course he felt bad, so to make him feel better
he sat down and ate her.
Then he ate his dad.

You'd have thought the episode would have left him disturbed,
but he was relatively unperturbed.
He reckons that life as an orphan is more fun.

There came a day when he needed some money to make his way
so he tried for council job on minimum pay,
but was considered too cruel and sadistic.
Even for Haringey.

Stan went ballistic.
He stuffed and mounted and buried an accountant
Then applied for the post of the guy he'd just killed.
But eventually gave up when they dug his grave up,
And discovered the vacancy was already filled

He was forced to resort to unutterable terror,
never squeaking a word so's to hide from detection
But then suddenly, due to an administrative error,
he was appointed Head of Child Protection.

Kissing application

Kiss me like you want me,
like you want to show me what you've got.
Kiss me like you've just been labelled tame
and need to prove you're not.
Kiss me luscious like it thrills you,
Kiss delicious like it fills you with fizz,
Ms. . . . and this is where you fill in your name

Kiss me gracefully at first
then every second kiss disgracefully
in an overly keen wench-quenching-her-thirst kind of way.
Kiss me now today like you mean it.
Kiss me like you've seen it done by dirty dancers.
Kiss me like you're passing me the answers to a quiz, Ms. . . .
this is where you tell me what your name is

Kiss me with abandon - frenzied kissing,
like husband and wife, newly wed,
still in bed practising the kiss of life, swapping tips
of tongues and eager lips
And digging nails in . . .
Hurry up, fill your details in.

Kiss me in a bout of passion, like it's going out of fashion.
kiss me like you're on a mission in a kissing competition.
Kiss me like I've just kidnapped your handsome
Kids, and kissing me's the ransom.

Hey, let's plan some arty rendezvous - say me and you Meander
through Vienna to a gallery -
And turn into some burnt sienna tinted allegory. . .
Picture The Kiss - soft surrender wrapped in gold and mint.
That tender mouth against her cradled face
Eclipsed by paint brushed lips.

How blissful rapture must have felt
as she knelt, for Gustav Klimt to capture,
Or just reclining naked. Mind you make it
more gentle than Auguste Rodin's ornamental kiss . . .
My dear madam, miss, mizz, - whatever you name is.

Kiss me senseless again and again in a wanton wet attack.
I'm not defenceless.
Tell me your name, and I bet I'll kiss you back.

Valentine

Your dreds are rastafarian
Your head is Presbyterian
Your arse is such a hairy one
Please say that you'll be mine

Your social skill's incompetent
your cooking leaves me wanting and
you're borderline incontinent
But I don't really mind

Your love of flowers and glitter is
As sickly sweet as licorice
But no one's found your clitoris,
You need to make a sign.

Your cuffs don't match your collar and
Your mum's lactose intolerant
But I will scream and holler until
you're my valentine

Going incremental

There's something a tiny bit different.
Changing nightly and day after day.
It's deteriorating ever so slightly
In a hideously subtle way
that's so insidious, it's invisible to us.
Sneaking up on us from behind.
By this time next year I'm going to be
completely out of my mind.

I'm going incremental.
You'll hardly notice that my cloak is
More disguise than ornamental
Hiding each degree that surreptitiously
Curves gently round at glacial trend
I'm gradually going round the bend
The voices in my head say 'eventually can not be curbed'
I'm incrementally disturbed.

We might bump into each other
You'll say 'Hey there - Whaddya know?'
I'll say 'I'm keeping it together'
You'll see - I've been letting myself go
But you've had time to contrast and compare
while I've been lying myself barefaced,
up too close to all the tiny steps -
to see they form a spiral staircase

Yep, I'm going incremental.
You won't notice that my coat is
More disguise than ornamental
But the signs collect imperceptibly
They form a list. How inept of me
As I teeter temperamentally, Alan's
incrementally unbalanced.

ANTONI GAUDÍ

Howdy, Gaudí
Proud designer logo donor
To Barcelona.
I suspect ya Architecture
maybe a Little rowdy even for Saudi Arabia.
Luckily your fame in Spain remains undiminished.
Shame you'll never get to see the finished
Sagrada Familia,
Will ya?

BRIAN COX

In his gentle Oldham accent
Brian Cox said quite by accident
we all coalesced from a collapsing cloud of dust

And I guessed it must be true,
although, he also said he knew
that things could only get better
But I kind of get a feeling
that we might have reached the ceiling.

LAUREN LAVERNE

Lauren Laverne
has voiced her concern
that nothing rhymes with oranges.
Pay her no mind -
I think you'll find that Lauren jus'
does.

The right to remain silent

And it goes without saying
You have the right to remain silent
Heaven knows disobeying whoever
Might turn the game violent
First they read you their rights
Then they send you the bill
For their god-given poetic licence to kill
It's an ill wind that blows up the bridge
To the edge of an island
And it goes without saying
You have the right to remain silent

And it goes without saying
You have the right to remain deluded
As you serve out the sentence that ends
'Service isn't included'
And they said that the ceiling
Is hung by a thread
But the crystal glass chandeliers
Beg for more lead
To illuminate signs that warn
'Give Way' exactly like you did
And it goes without saying
You have the right to remain deluded

And it goes without saying
You have the right to remain silent
But it's hard to complain
When you're caught in the reign of a tyrant

Malignant narcissist

The wreckers have stolen the glow from the lighthouse
and beckoned a moron into the White House
with a synapse lapse as thick as a brick shite house.

A menace, a misogynist,
All nescience and artifice,
this ignorant malignant narcissist
pisses on your territory and marks it his.
He cocks his leg outside his jurisdiction,
urinating on the Press and Constitution.

He's the Nazi apologist, incoherent and woolly.
The vindictive drunk, the playground bully,
not fully in control of his faculties.
Reality, detractors and facts – he can't tackle these.
This tangerine tan with a nicotine mantelpiece.
Illiterate self-serving undeserving bragger.
This maniac, this monster, this pussy grabber
remains unreachable, unimpeachable,
as long as all the suckers protect the orange fucker.

And still the idiot blurts out gibberish and mystery
as the mounting death toll adds to his legacy.
The dumbest president in all of history.

I wrote this poem when I was a little bit pissed.
I think you'll soon spot, it's not so much a poem, as a list.
A long catalogue of song titles, twisted around
Until each name sounds the same as a make of car.
A bizarre and pointless mission to chart the position
of 20 hit recordings according to their automobility.
Facilitated by jars of ale, and sparked off by talking back at Alexi Sayle's song
Ello John, got a new motor?
Yes, actually. As a matter of fact Alexi, I've got - quite a few, Though to
be honest, it has to be said, they're all in my head.

I close my eyelids, and make up hybrids, like Brian Hyland's
Mitsubishi teeny weeny yellow potent Lamborghini.

So here's the chart, starting at

Number 20, Kylie Minogue - Can't get you Audi my head.

At 19 it's Bob Marley and the Wailers - No woman no Chrysler

At 18 David Bowie - John, I'm only Datsun

Madonna at 17 - Like a Peugeot, touched for the very first time

George Michael at 16 - Last Christmas I gave Yamaha

At 15 it's Arctic Monkeys - I bet you look good Honda Dance floor.

14, The Commodores - You're once, twice, three times a Lada.

13, Marvin Gaye - Where Chevrolet my hat that's my home.

Bonnie Tyler at 12 - Toyota clips of the heart.

At 11 it's Lesley Gore - Mazerrati, and I'll cry if I want to

The motorcar-tastic top ten kicks off with

Jimmy Cliff - Granada they come – Granada they fall.

9, Otis Redding - Citroen on the dock of the bay.

At 8, it's Whitney Huston – Hy . . undai undai undai will always love you

7, Kaizer Chiefs - I predict a Fiat

At 6, George Harrison - While my big car, Bentley, weeps

5, Judy Garland - Somewhere Rover the rainbow

4, Kings of Leon - My Lexus on fire.

3, Eminem - Will the real Mercedes please stand up

2, Gerry & the Pacemakers - You'll never Vauxhall lone

And in the true tradition of every chart countdown that's ever been,
the obligatory number one belongs to Queen with Bohemian Rhapsody

(Is this the real life is this just fantasy - Cortina landslide –
no escape from reality)

L.O.N.D.O.N. ***('Ello Wendy Owen)***

'Ello Wendy Owen,
There's a whole lot goin' on.
See her throng and swarm and hurry.
Inner London, north of Surrey.
She's a winner east of Pinner,
West of Thurrock, thorough fuck-up

'Ello Wendy Owen,
River splits in equal parts.
Wendy Owen, left of Essex,
Right of Windsor, south of Herts.
Up the East end, down the West end,
Public places, private parts.

'Ello Wendy Owen.
Singing 'Ello Wendy Owen.
Singing 'Ello Wendy Owen,
Sat inside the bendy goin'
Round in circles, round forever,
Destined never to arrive.
Territorial tar necklace
Hard shoulder length M25.

Multi cultural, multi sculptural,
Fit for richest, fit for poorest.
Tower blocked and Semi detached,
And terraced, and terrorist, and tourist.

Talking Cockney, Sloan or City.
Es-tu-ary, norf an sarf.
You avin' a giraffe? You avin' a Gerald Scarfe?
You avin' a bubble? You're avin' a laugh!
Aint cha? aint cha? Ancient and modern.
Victorian, Edwardian, sun baked, or sodden.

There's the racket of the traffic
Siren wail Big Issue bellow,
And the Metropolitan policeman never says
'Ello 'ello 'ello

'Ello Wendy Owen
Singing 'Ello Wendy Owen
Singing 'Ello Wendy Owen
Sat inside the bendy goin'
round in circles, round forever
destined never to arrive.
Wendy owen wears a necklace,
Hard shoulder length M25.

September the central heatingth

An indoor woolly jumper and hat.
A hovering hand on the thermostat.
Is Autumn taunting Summer to vacate?
You're trying hard not to capitulate,
But the boiler's winking and flashing its switch,
And whispering 'push my button bitch'.
And you press your finger - and summer has gone
The moment you turn the heating on.

Perhaps I'm collapsing in love

It started with a tic.

Intermittent.

Sporadic.

A bit of a fit at the flick of a twitch.
The kind of spasm with which junkies are afflicted
- Brad Pitt has 'em in 12 Monkeys
I should've predicted
I was going to get sick

It's hardly romantic
My breathing's erratic
My pulse rate is static,
My blood pressure's diving
I'm cracked in the attic
I'm barely surviving
My speech is impeded
More oxygen's needed
My heartbeat's in prolapse
Defeat is conceded

Perhaps I'm collapsing in love

My temperature's climbing
And soon the room I'm in
Is tumbling and spinning,
My headaches are blinding
My focus is blurred,
And my words are beginning
To turn out all slurred
And absurd and unheard of
Cos speaking in tongues
Isn't one of my talents

My lung's a bit missing
You're witnessing Alan's
Entire loss of balance,
Entire loss of feeling.
Precarious keeling
And everything's re-bounding
right off the ceiling
and falling back down in
A plummeting climax
Before it all blacks out
My life flashes past
All the great and the ghastly
The highs and catastrophes
Triumphs and craps

Yes perhaps I'm collapsing in love

Then somebody spoke :
And said 'Hey - it's OK -
You're just having a stroke'

Chat-up star

Seize upon astrology
with no hint of apology
for this presumptuous chat-up carpe diem.

Get in with this bizarre line -
"I bet I can tell your star sign
simply by the taste of your perineum"

Paraprosdokian

A paraprosdokian is a statement whose latter part is surprising or unexpected in a way that makes you reinterpret the first part. Comedians call it 'Pull back and reveal'. Well known songs may have turned out quite differently if their opening lines were a paraprosdokian.

Little Richard:
I woke up this morning. Lucille was not in sight.
But then I pulled back the duvet and there she was.

The Human league:
You were working as a waitress in a cocktail bar
and yet according to our records you haven't declared any of your earnings for this period, or paid national Insurance.

Dolly Parton:
Jolene, Jolene, Jolene,
JOLENE!
Oh I'm terribly sorry, I though you were Jolene.

The Carpenters:
Why do birds suddenly appear
Every time you are near? Perhaps you smell of worms.

Paul McCartney:
Yesterday . . . . .Or was it the day before?
D'you know I think it might have been Wednesday . .

Roy Orbison:
A candy-coloured clown they call the sandman, tiptoes to my room every night.
Turns out my uncle Reg isn't my real uncle.

Elvis Presley
We're caught in a trap.
I can't walk out. I HATE revolving doors.

Elton John:
It's a little bit funny, this feeling inside.
Can't work out how you manage a prostate examination with both hand on my shoulders.

Carly Simon:
You walked into the party, like you were walking onto a yacht.
I mean, who wears a yellow oilskin sou'wester to a black tie memorial do?

Robert Palmer:
Your lights are on, but you're not home.
I reckon you must have gone out and left the lights on.

Aretha Franklin:
The moment I wake up, before I put on my make up,
I have a really good shit.

Jimi Hendrix:
There must be some kind of way out of here.
Probably the same door I came in through.

Simon & Garfunkle:
Hello darkness my old friend. How's the family? How's Bleak, Dim, and Murky? And the kids - Shadow, Gloomy and Dull?

Pete Seeger:
If I had a hammer, I wouldn't have to go round singing 'If I had a hammer', because I'd HAVE a hammer and I'd shut the fuck up about it.

The Police
Roxanne, you don't have to put on the red light.
It's on a timer switch.

The Eagles
On a dark desert highway, cool breeze in my hair
and yet the SatNav insists we're in Dunstable town centre.

The twin mashed adjectives of Reykjavik

His invitation begged an alluring prospect.
He brought it with him to the imposing wrought iron gate.
He was late, and by now there was a sauntering crowd to negotiate.
Undaunted, he swung into attack.
From the edge he wedged and ducked and threaded his way,
like a rucksack through a hedge,
emerging dishevelled,
with his invitation bevelled,
but intact.

The crumpled note was written in lipstick.
He glanced at the cryptic instruction.
It read "Come mess beside the best qualified (adj.)"
He made his way into the hall,
wondering if he'd get to see her at all.

He would have been pleased to merely meet her,
But as soon as he'd squeezed himself into the place
She appeared out of nowhere - right up in his face.
First a few inches, then a millimetre.
Wham-bam-boozled man!
Suddenly it seemed she was right there,
like she must have - beamed up from somewhere.

He felt concussed by this entirely beguiling
and utterly indescribable vision.
She severed connectors with the precision of an archer,
leaving wonder and marvel to flood the vacuum
left by comprehension's departure.

Close up, her eyes were the mist and mystery of undiscovered planets.
Her face, her shoulders, her whole body was woven
with notions of alien emotions, equally gripping and repulsive,
all at once evocative, exquisite, exotic, and grotesque -
like those amorphous creatures at the bottom of the ocean.

He steadied himself against a desk.
This was uncharted topography, unfeasible geometry,
like greeting a completely new colour in an unrealised spectrum.

She was more or less than a confession of the recollections of every
beautiful woman he could remember, but for the present
he was bereft of perception, and language had left him.
It was as though she had stolen all the descriptive words
he'd ever heard of.

She pursed her lips
like she was about to kiss him.
So he pursed his lips too,
But she was just forming a W.
She said what sounded like 'Wood?'
He suddenly noticed a hint of unwrinkling
and the inkling of an erection.
She went on
'- you like to see my collection of adjectives?'

Now, he came from the suburbs, surrounded by nouns
and encircled by verbs.
He was curious to see how the other half lives.
Then she added 'Some of them are superlatives . . . Come
follow me and see the marvelest on display'
He swallowed hard and said 'Which way?'

She grabbed his tie, spun round on her heels
and towed him along over her shoulder, away from the crowd
to the ornamental gates of the great atrium.
Once inside they were alone with only the echo of their footsteps.
On the floor stretched out before them was a vast grid
of glass lidded display tables.

Row upon row of long mahogany framed cabinets
full of neatly arranged adjectives: Substantive, attributive, predicative,
eponymous, absolute, irregular and florid.
Each nestled on its own plush velvet cushion, beneath a spotlight
fanfare celebrating its adjectival arrival.

He couldn't make out if they were ordered poetically
or alphabetically. Succulent next to Truculent, Anal and Banal together.
Leathery and Feathery, Specious and Facetious,
Empurpled and Platonic,
and ironically Heretical next to Alphabetical.

As he wove his way between rhyme and reason,
there was an awkward moment when he caught himself
inadvertently straddling Visceral and Swollen.
He threw away a hasty 'How exactly did you get all of these?'
She seemed pleased with a nonchalant
'Oh - they're mostly stolen.'

Then she insisted they make their way to her pièce de résistance.
She led him through inter-leading doors to the mezzanine floors
of the interlocking hall of mirror image contradicting adjectives.

The onomatopoeic appeared to neatly fit
Behind the heterologic - words that sound quite the opposite.

Overhead hung a notice, and written upon it: 'Bucolic
has something of a plague about it
but depicts rural meadows and hedges and trees While
Nosopoetic sounds tellingly lyrical
but means the ability to make diseases'

She seizes his hand and points to the grand staircase sweeping up to her
prize exhibit, and they slowly make their way
to the elaborate antechamber of the sculpted sanctum.

Towering above the packed cabinets stands
the altar of the precious, the pinnacle, the climactic artefact.

And there - there atop two onyx columns set upon a marble plinth they
gently breathed, sheathed in thick Corinthian capitals of glistening aspic . . .
The Mighty Twin Mashed Adjectives of Reykjavik,
I d y l l i q u i d and **L i q u i d y l l i c**

He gazed, amazed at the fluency and symmetry,
the numinous fusion.
'Are they alive? I think I can see them moving'
She nodded, amused.
'Of course. Sometimes they glow and hiss'
He was intrigued by something gorgeous leaking from the phonics
onto the onyx pillar.
'What's all that 'oozing down the fluting' about?' 'That' she
said 'is liquid bliss.
Sometimes it comes shooting out.'

He couldn't see her, but he could sense she was standing to his rear.
He fixed his stare straight ahead at the two idyllic liquid taijitu,
and said 'I guess you need to feed them?'

There was a pause, but from behind his back he recognised the sound
clothes make when they slide down and drop to the floor -
A muffled hiss and crumpled flap,

Eventually she said 'Absolutely.'
Then, with a sublime whisper '...Yes feeding time' Followed by the
soft brush of falling negligee against skin as it sank around her ankles.
He was without a doubt aware of the stepping out of underwear -
A sort of quiet gliss.

'What do you feed them on?' he asked.

She said 'This.'

Complaints

The Shard isn't tall enough
Micro chips aren't small enough
A schism isn't wide enough
I'm bound to be not tied enough
Tony Blair's not tried enough
Thatcher hasn't died enough
Boris is a liar, enough
To set his pants on fire.

A vampire isn't bitten enough
A kitten isn't cuddly enough
A pavement isn't puddly enough
Confusion isn't muddily enough
Birmingham isn't Dudley enough
Dudley isn't Moore than enough

Breakfast isn't fast enough
A shelf life doesn't last enough
A light year isn't far enough
A smart car isn't car enough
Macabre isn't 'Noir' enough
The latest thing's not Quoi de neuf

Poets don't get paid enough
and plastic won't degrade enough
Spouses don't get laid enough
A crevice isn't niche enough
A hookah isn't sheesh enough
A sheesha isn't bong enough
A penis isn't dong enough
Underpants aren't thong enough
A piece of string's not long enough
A hawser isn't strong enough
Two wrongs don't make a right enough
Two Wrights don't pioneer flight enough

A synapse isn't quick enough
A bigot isn't thick enough
Persistence doesn't try enough
Existence isn't why enough
A ceasefire doesn't hold enough
A bowler hat's not bold enough
A fluffer isn't buff enough
And passion isn't rough enough
Substantive isn't stuff enough
And I can't tell when enough's enough
So I'll stop.

Alvinophilia
(Belly button fetish)

She loves me
She loves me knot

The station is leaving the train

That midday solstice sun will be as bright
as it's ever going to get,
on the longest day, and the shortest night.
And yet - it isn't.
It's not even risen. Or set.

It's doing nothing at all,
except for being the brilliant fiery ball it always is.
Just sitting there. Centre stage.
All fabulous and fizz, while we fidget about with our seating
arrangements, obtuse perspectives, and proscenium tangents.

We observe from the front row, circle and gods,
Below the equator, or up North and at odds
with that obdurate object, obstinately fixed,
while our shadows move around us between and betwixt.

And the sun cares not a spot of its nuclear fusion
for our ozone, carbon, and greenhouse collusion,
or our time of day or month or season.
It just shines for all time with no rhyme or reason.

The fact is, what the solstice celebration lacks is
how indifferent the sun is to our orbit and axis.
and our inclination to sashay about the vertical plane while
imagining the station is leaving the train.

Wave your hands in the air like you just don't care

Ever since Cameo's 'Word up' immortalised the rallying cry 'Wave your hands in the air like you just don't care.' it continues to turn up in songs and stage shouts.
Here are some alternatives that might be considered with a more nuanced approach to how much of a fuck you're prepared to give.

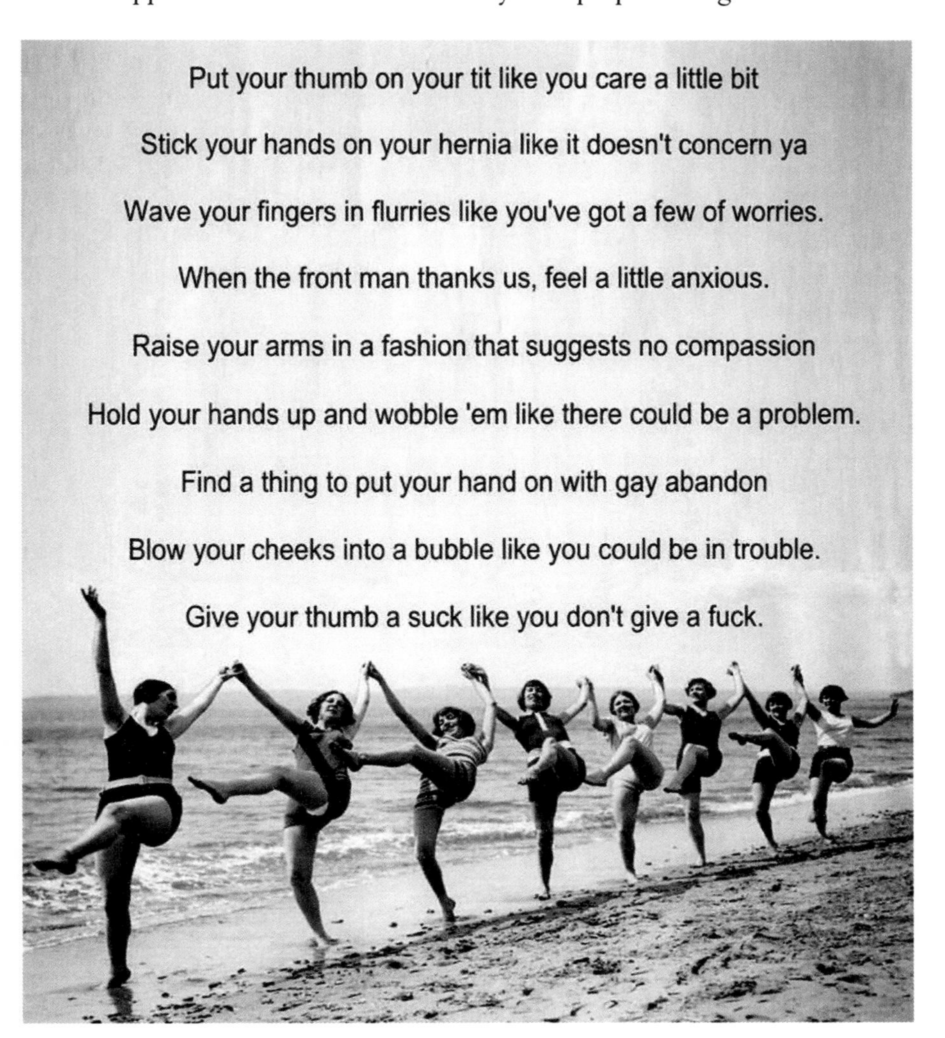